ALLIED BATTLE TANKS

WESTERN TANK UNITS ON THE CENTRAL EUROPEAN FRONTIER

TEXT AND PHOTOS BY

YVES DEBAY

Printed in Italy

Windrow & Greene

London

THE TANK — A WORLD OF ITS OWN

The front cover shows a platoon of the latest model of Leopard — Leo 2 A4 — equipped with ultra-sophisticated fire controls, and protected by Chobham armour. These tanks serve with West Germany's Panzerbataillon 284 from 10 Panzerdivision, based at Ulm.

(Opposite) Commander of an M41 of the Danish Guard Hussars, liberally camouflaged.

(Below) A Panzer crew from PzBn.293, 10 PzDiv. enjoy a moment of relaxation during exercise 'Kolibri 86'.

When night falls, and the battlefield becomes still, the tired footslogger scrapes himself a foxhole and curls up in it. The armoured cavalry trooper has other things to think about: tensioning a track, checking fluid levels, stocking up with fuel and ammunition — like his horse-mounted ancestor, his golden rule remains '*First, care for your mount*'. Only after his heavy work is done can he enjoy for a few hours the tankman's great advantage over the infantryman — warmth! While the muddy hole-dweller shivers in his clammy sleeping bag, the trooper stretches out on the warm engine deck of his steel monster like a medieval peasant on his tiled stove. With the cannon traversed to 'six o'clock' as a ridge-pole, he can even make a snug tent with a tarpaulin.

And when morning breaks, a jerrycan cunningly placed in a corner of the engine compartment provides instant hot water for shaving. The English 'tanky' can even offer the visitor a mug of hot tea, thanks to the built-in cooker in his Challenger; while a Belgian lancer will produce a can of beer, since the standard size exactly fits the machine gun ammunition stowage of his Leopard.

But however they prize their small comforts, the tank troopers are ready to go into combat faithful to the old cavalry traditions and trusting in their star. Confident in their skills and their machines, they pretend to forget that they risk perhaps the worst death of all — trapped in a blazing inferno. Whether or not their luck holds, they know that they will make the enemy pay dearly, and that the crew will exper-

ience the strange drunkenness of battle — '. . . *when you're firing, and the smell of cordite fills the turret, mixed with the smell of hot oil, when the radio crackles ceaselessly, and the commander bellows his orders* . . .'

A tank is, essentially, four young men, usually between 18 and 30 years old. In their turret they have no room for formality: they live together, eat together, and, if war comes, they may die together. You might hear a corporal cheerfully abusing a lieutenant; you'll often see a tank commander kicking the gunner crouched below him; but this is a team, welded together by the knowledge that in battle one man's mistake can mean instant death for the whole crew.

Technically, these are 'state-of-the-art' soldiers, operating laser-beams, thermal imagers, passive light intensification sights, and a whole range of other ultra-sophisticated equipment. But in spirit they remain fiercely proud of their ancient identities: as hussars, cuirassiers, dragoons, lancers, lifeguards — or simply, 'cav'. The Germans, despite the austere anonymity of their numbered *Panzer* battalions, preserve the old heraldry in the elaborate decorations of regimental beer mugs. The Americans still sometimes wear Stetsons with crossed sabre badges; the British unselfconsciously invoke the memory of the Light Brigade at Balaclava, and the French, the trumpets of Murat.

If they are proud of their traditions, they are equally protective about their machines. Each believes that *his* tank is the best — and in a sense each is right, because machinery is nothing if the spirit is lacking.

IS THE TANK DEAD?

The elephant's graveyard: near the notorious 'Chinese Farm' position in the Sinai Desert the gutted hulks of an Israeli Centurion and (inset) an Egyptian T-55 bear mute witness to the savagery of the 1973 Yom Kippur War, the greatest clashes of armour since Kursk, 1943.

In October 1973 Egyptian infantry crossed the Suez Canal in force, and overran the Israeli positions of the Bar Lev Line. Caught off guard, the Israelis counter-attacked at once with their tank battalions — the spearhead of the IDF, which in the past had always ensured victory. In a blinding dust cloud two armoured brigades sped towards the Egyptian penetrations — and in two hours fell back, terribly mauled. Without the close support of their own infantry, the Centurions and M48s were turned into blazing torches by the wire-guided 'Sagger' missiles and RPG-7 rocket launchers of elusive teams of highly trained Egyptian infantry. It was a black day for *Tsahal*; and military pundits were quick to predict the death of the main battle tank as an independent arm of warfare.

Two days later the Egyptians, in their turn, launched an armoured assault in the Sinai. By now Israel had mobilised her reserves; and the world held its breath as the greatest concentration of tanks since the battle of Kursk in 1943 manoeuvred for advantage. For two days the desert thundered and blazed; and gradually the superior technical skills of the Israelis turned the tide — though at terrible cost.

Suddenly, the IDF found the weak point between two Egyptian units; once more their tanks drove forward, exploiting the penetration. Once more they raged through the enemy's rear areas, blasting with 105mm shells the missile sites which had denied freedom of action over the battlefield to Israeli jets. The

pundits had been too hasty: the main battle tank was not yet destined to join the obsolete hardware gathering dust in military museums.

Nevertheless, the 1973 war affected the operational doctrine of the world's armoured units profoundly. The days of great tank thrusts, ranging freely over the terrain, seemed over. On modern battlefields alive with anti-tank weapons the tanks needed the protection of accompanying mechanised infantry as never before. But the tank still remained, and will remain for the foreseeable future, the decisive 'breakthrough' weapon — the rôle for which it had been created during the First World War.

PASSIVE ARMOUR

Armour is what turns a piece of mobile artillery into an assault weapon — a tank. Armour itself is constantly evolving, and so are the weapons designed to penetrate it. The 'guns and armour race', as each design bureau works to achieve a temporary advantage, is as ceaseless as the medieval struggle for dominance between bowyers, archery tacticians, and the makers of suits of plate.

Today three main types of 'passive' armour are in use: the classic 'homogenous' armour, 'spaced' armour, and 'composite' armour.

Homogenous armour — steel plate — is as old as the tank itself, and characterised every generation of tanks up to the Chieftain, Leopard 1 and M60, which will doubtless be the last to rely upon it. It gives good protection against kinetic energy projectiles, but is vulnerable to the new APFSDS rounds — 'armour piercing fin stabilised discarding sabot'. Even though conventionally armoured tanks can still resist frontal hits from shaped charge weapons such as the RPG-7, they are increasingly vulnerable to lateral strikes by modern AT weapons. In 1987 the Chadian forces destroyed large numbers of Libyan T-55 and T-62 tanks by flank attacks with French-supplied Milan missiles.

The sheer weight of homogenous armour is also a handicap. It requires a trade-off between mobility and protection, or new and fuel-hungry engines. In the Second World War the super-armoured 76-ton 'King Tiger' was slow, limited by its appetite for scarce fuel, and unable to use most bridges; against this, in suitable terrain a King Tiger could often destroy six Shermans or T-34s before succumbing to massed attack.

Spaced armour dates from the Second World War. To ward off shaped charges and anti-tank shot the Germans mounted extra steel plates on frames around the turrets and hulls of *Panzer* III and IV tanks, leaving a space between this external armour and the integral armour. This simple system slowed or prematurely detonated anti-tank projectiles before they hit the vehicle. Though now much more sophisticated, armour using this basic principle is incorporated into the design of today's Leopard 1 A1, Israeli Merkava and Chieftain Mk.15 tanks.

For security reasons many details of the latest 'composite' armours remain unknown. This system, which protects today's 'second generation' of tanks, was developed at the end of the 1960s by Britain's Royal Armament Research and Development Establishment near Chobham in Surrey, and is popularly termed 'Chobham armour'. The system was tested on the Chieftain, and the Challenger was the first operational tank to incorporate it. The Leopard 2 and M1 Abrams followed suit; and the USSR, which has certainly acquired the secret, seems to have installed comparable armour on late model T-72 and T-80 tanks.

Basically, composite armour is a 'sandwich' composed of successive layers of steel, rubber and ceramic materials. This channels and neutralises the effects of shaped charge AT missiles, and gives good, though not decisive protection against the latest kinetic energy projectiles. Certain alarmist reports have even claimed that the latest T-80s are practically invulnerable to missiles such as Milan and Dragon; but this is impossible, if only because its bulk and weight means that composite armour can only be used on the 'frontal quadrant' and not all round the tank.

ACTIVE ARMOUR

During the Israeli invasion of Lebanon in 1982 military observers remarked upon the fact that vital areas of IDF Centurions, M48s and M60s were covered with strange external 'boxes'. These proved to be a novel form of protection code-named 'Blazer' — an 'active' or 'reactive' armour in the form of explosive blocks.

As already mentioned, the Israeli tank brigades suffered very heavy losses in the 1973 Yom Kippur War from shaped charge AT missiles, both wire-guided 'Saggers' and shoulder-fired RPG projectiles. Foreseeing that in any invasion of Lebanon their tanks would be faced by large numbers of such weapons, the IDF adopted a novel counter-device. This was simply

(Right) 'Blazer'-type active armour fitted to an M60 A1 of the US Marine Corps — the first Western tanks to adopt this controversial system after the Israelis.

(Below) Chieftain Mk.15 of 5th Royal Inniskilling Dragoon Guards — the 'Skins'. Chieftains were the first tanks to be fitted with the new generation of Chobham composite armour, and the whole series were an example of the choice of protection and firepower over mobility.

a small explosive charge placed between two sheets of a special alloy and placed in a metal 'box'. The shape of the boxes varied according to the position in which they were bolted to the tank armour.

The principle was simplicity itself. When a shaped charge weapon hit one of the boxes it would explode, and the explosion would diffuse the tongue of flame from the shaped charge before it could penetrate the main armour.

During the 1982 'Peace for Galilee' operation the Syrians recovered knocked-out IDF tanks fitted with 'Blazer'; and before long Soviet tanks were also appearing under a rash of 'boxes'. The US Marines have also adopted reactive armour for their M60 A1s. It has disadvantages, however: it is a 'once only' protection, and dangerous for accompanying infantry and exposed crews. Reports that some Soviet tanks had been fitted with multi-layer active armour seems to have been deliberate 'disinformation' planted on technically naive observers: successive layers would all explode when the outer layer detonated.

FIRE CONTROLS

M1 Abrams tanks of the US 66th Armored Regiment, 3rd Infantry Division utilising their remarkable fire controls during the Canadian Army Trophy firing competitions, 1987.

The first post-war generation of tanks aimed their guns by means of simple optical telescopes. The gunner had to be able to estimate range quickly before opening fire. Only exceptional training or luck brought a first-shot hit; often the gunner had to fire and correct several times, wasting time and revealing his position. Some improved optical range-finder sights derived from photographic image-coincidence technology improved accuracy, but not speed. Neither did such sights take account of such vital factors as windspeed, propellant temperature, muzzle velocity, or the angle of the tank. They also required extensive crew training for effective use.

The British found a temporary solution by mounting a conventional machine gun alongside the guns of the Centurion and Chieftain. A short burst of tracer at the target allowed easy visual correction of aim; but this simple, practical method suffered from slowness, and lack of range — the main gun had a range far beyond the machine gun's 1,800 yards.

The appearance of the laser range-finder at the end of the 1960s revolutionised tank gunnery. The press of a button sent a laser beam to the target and back at the speed of light; and automatic calculation of elapsed time gave an immediate and accurate range reading. Laser range-finders were soon coupled to on-board computers, the whole assembly being termed 'fire controls'. The computer reconciles the information provided by various sensors mounted in the turret and by the laser range-finder, calculating the best angle of fire.

The Belgian SABCA fire controls used in the Belgian, Canadian and Australian Leopard 1 have seven sensors giving readings of ambient temperature, propellant temperature, wind, atmospheric pressure, degree of barrel wear, angle of tank, and turret movements. All this information is reconciled in the gunner's aiming binoculars as an aiming point or luminous cross: he simply places this on the target and fires, with a (theoretical) 99.8% chance of a first-shot hit.

Such revolutionary fire controls as the SABCA, the British IFCS, the French COBELCA, and similar American and Soviet equipment allow extraordinary speed and accuracy. Today a trained crew can engage and destroy six enemy tanks in a minute (under range conditions, at least). During trials one Chieftain crew using IFCS scored nine hits in under 53 seconds.

The M1 Abrams, Challenger and Leopard 2 are also fitted with the very latest, and very costly, thermal imaging equipment. This picks up the differences in infrared radiation between a 'hot' tank and the 'cold' background. It literally enables a tank gunner to 'see' his target night or day, in any weather, even through a smoke screen. The advantage enjoyed by a tank commander equipped with thermal imaging over an enemy without it can hardly be exaggerated.

ARMAMENT AND AMMUNITION

The first tanks were conceived during the First World War, to accompany the waves of assault infantry who could not penetrate, unaided, the twin barriers of barbed wire and machine gun fire. These tanks were in fact nothing more than mobile, lightly armoured artillery pieces; some, indeed, were armed only with machine guns. In the generations since 1918 tank-versus-tank fighting has led to a progressive increase in the power of tank guns. Today the main battle tank (MBT) is equipped with a high-performance cannon, and with two machine guns: one, mounted co-axially with the cannon, for close range defence, and one 'superstructure' gun mounted on the turret top for anti-aircraft defence.

Since 1945 the main tank gun has evolved considerably. The Pattons, Centurions and T-55s in service during the 1960s were armed with guns of 90mm to 100mm calibre. The generation of tanks designed during that decade generally adopted the 105mm gun, notably the excellent British L-7 gun which equipped most NATO tanks. The latest main battle tanks use 120mm weapons: the L-11 in the Challenger, and the Rheinmetall 120mm smooth-bore gun in the Leopard 2 and the M1 Abrams. The Soviet T-64, T-72 and T-80 use a 125mm smooth-bore gun designated D-81(2A46). The different types of ammunition fired by these guns are described below under their NATO designations:
— HE (High Explosive), used against infantry and unprotected targets.
— HEAT (High Explosive Anti-Tank), a shaped charge shell. When this hits the target it detonates in such a way as to send a thin tongue of flame blasting through the armour; semi-molten metal flies off inside, and the temperature inside the target tank rises instantaneously to some 2000°, exploding stored ammunition.
— APDS and APFSDS (Armour Piercing Discarding Sabot, Armour Piercing Fin Stabilised Discarding Sabot). Kinetic energy shells, using a small core projectile of extremely hard metal — forms of tungsten or uranium — surrounded by a sabot or 'shoe' of full cannon calibre, fired at very high velocity by large, powerful propellant charges. The 'dart' itself penetrates the target's armour and destroys it by internal ricochet. Kinetic energy shells can penetrate the brittle ceramic plates used in composite armours, whose 'sandwich' of other materials is thus necessary to stop them.

Neither shaped charge nor kinetic rounds can guarantee penetration; and no type of armour can guarantee protection.

THE FIRING SEQUENCE:

1 — The tank commander chooses a target and designates it to the gunner, who lays the main gun.

2 — On the tank commander's order, the loader takes the designated round of ammunition, e.g. HEAT, and loads it into the breech. By pressing a button he signals 'ready to fire'. The gunner presses a button corresponding to HEAT ammunition, and activates the laser range-finder by another button, while keeping the graticule of his sights lined up on the target.

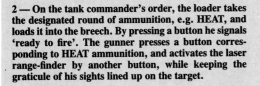
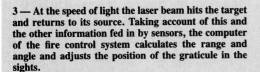

HEAT

3 — At the speed of light the laser beam hits the target and returns to its source. Taking account of this and the other information fed in by sensors, the computer of the fire control system calculates the range and angle and adjusts the position of the graticule in the sights.

4 — The gunner re-centres the sights on the target, and shouts 'Ready!'

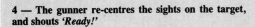

5 — On the tank commander's order, or on his own initiative if so instructed, the gunner fires.

6 — The target destroyed, the crew search for a second target. The entire sequence can be completed in ten seconds by any well trained crew.

(Right) Two HEAT shells and a rapier-pointed APFSDS round displayed in front of an AMX-30 tank of France's 5th Cuirassiers. (Left) A young conscript from a 1st Chasseurs AMX-30 crew manhandling a 105mm shell — the blue head identifies a drill round.

13

THE TANK'S ENEMIES

The best way to kill a tank is with another tank. But no army can anticipate having tanks in place to oppose any given enemy thrust; and all armies spend much time, money and ingenuity on providing a wide range of anti-tank weapons.

THE TANK DESTROYER

Wheeled or tracked vehicles equipped with AT missiles are in service with the AT companies of armoured and mechanised divisions. These low-profile vehicles can engage enemy tanks at 4,000 yards; they are generally employed on the flanks of major armoured units. Fairly lightly protected, they are vulnerable to tank guns and to field artillery.

VAB HOT of France's 1st Chasseurs.

THE ANTI-TANK HELICOPTER

Today a 'flying armoured vehicle' itself, the anti-tank helicopter is deadly. Mobile in three dimensions, it can lurk stationary below a crest or behind a wood to search out its prey. Tank crews, deafened by their engine, their radio traffic and the screeching of their tracks, cannot hear the helicopter. At the last moment it can bob up into line-of-sight, fire self-guiding 'fire-and-forget' missiles, and duck away. Lightly armoured vehicles can be engaged directly with its automatic cannon.

But the helicopter is also vulnerable, if it is once spotted. Branches agitated by its rotors can betray its hiding place, and a shell fired into the trees will tear it out of the sky; light automatic fire can also be deadly, although modern helicopters have survived surprisingly heavy damage from small arms.

Above all the helicopter has the advantage of range: it can fire missiles at 4,000 yards, while the effective range of the MBT in broken, crowded Central European terrain is seldom above 2,000 yards.

AIR POWER

History provides many instances of armoured thrusts halted, even annihilated by air attack: against bombs, rockets and napalm the tank is helpless unless protected by its own air support. Both America and the USSR have developed specialised 'tank-killer' aircraft — the A-10 Thunderbolt II, and the Sukhoi Su-27 'Frogfoot' — festooned with missiles and mounting super-fast automatic cannon.

Soviet Sukhoi SU-27 attack aircraft.

THE INFANTRY ANTI-TANK MISSILE

Thanks to this type of weapon, which is light, accurate, easy to use, and powerful, the modern infantryman can destroy a million-dollar tank at 2,000 yards. The widely-used Milan and the American TOW have both proved themselves in battle. Both are highly mobile, and can be mounted on a jeep or other all-terrain vehicle. A solid hit is deadly to most tanks, and even the latest, most sophisticated armour is no absolute protection.

British LAW-90 84mm rocket launcher.

ARTILLERY AND MINES

Both types of weapon have always been able to slow down tank advances, without stopping them. Improvements continue all the time, however, such as the American 'Copperhead' shell; the fire of a conventional artillery battery equipped with these shells can be guided by a laser designator operated by a forward observer. A battery of NATO multiple rocket launchers can create a minefield from the air in a matter of moments, or shower an advancing tank force with thousands of small but deadly AT munitions.

American MLRS multiple rocket launcher, capable of firing thousands of sub-calibre munitions or of creating a minefield.

ROCKET LAUNCHERS

In the last resort, when practically at hand-to-hand range, the infantryman has a chance to destroy 'his' tank with a simple shoulder-fired rocket launcher, the descendant of the 'bazooka' and *Panzerfaust* of the Second World War. In open terrain he will very seldom have the chance; but in thick country or an urban setting a man with iron nerves can get the desired result. However, to do more than scratch the latest MBT armour the firer would have to place his shot very carefully in a vulnerable area, which means exposing himself for a suicidally long time.

15

THE CREW

The fighting compartment of a tank is a hideously cramped space, full of awkward, sharp-edged metal objects, and permeated by an indefinable stink made up of oil, explosive, and hydraulic fluid. Four men live, work, eat and often sleep here: their movements are ridiculously limited, and each has to make a constant effort not to provoke his mates. Murphy's Law ensures that if an open can of beans is put down anywhere, just once, then it will inevitably hide until it can turn upside down over the commander's map when next on the move . . . The crew must function as a team at all times; each man is responsible for all their lives, and a tank where there is bad feeling, or where one man hesitates over his duties, is a dead tank.

THE DRIVER

' . . . To steer this monster isn't always easy — 50 tons doesn't answer to the controls first time, like a kiddy-car. On manoeuvres outside camp I have to be careful all the time — get too free and easy and you can cause a lot of damage. You just have to *kiss* a wall, and it's goodbye wall. In theory the commander guides me — he's higher up and he can see better, and I have to trust him. But in combat, or any other situation where seconds count, I have to be able to act on my own initiative. If I saw a red ball flying towards us, for instance, that's an AT missile — and it would be up to me to take evasive action, but fast, and to get us into cover without stopping to ask permission from *anybody.*

'When we halt, it's always the same circus: check the levels, check the suspension, and retension the track if it needs it. When we fill up the other guys lend a hand, luckily — it takes a hell of a lot of jerrycans to shift a ton of juice!'

A hard winter for this British Scorpion CVRT driver of a recce unit.

THE GUNNER

'. . . It's all a question of reflexes. If I don't knock out an enemy tank first shot, he's going to have us. Above all, I have to spot him quickly, with my sighting equipment. As soon as the commander gives me a target I have to spot it, and get *on* it. Almost in the same second the commander tells me what ammo to use, and I have to hit the button straight away — the *right* button . . . If I select the wrong setting the shell could detonate 50 yards in front of the muzzle, because of the different ballistics of the different types of round. In a NATO competition that sort of mistake costs us a bottle of booze: in combat, it could blow away our supporting infantry . . . At night, I have to clean the barrel — and that's not a pop-gun out there! My mates give me a hand, though . . .'

Tankers of an Abrams crew from the US 70th Armor, 24th Inf.Div.; painted sand-colour for an exercise in Turkey, the tanks of this Georgia-based unit are earmarked to reinforce the Central European front in an emergency.

'In a combat situation I'd have to give instructions to the driver and the gunner, spot and engage the enemy, keep us screened from return fire, *and* maintain contact with the other tanks in the platoon. Communication has to be perfect. During a realistic battle exercise I'm on an incredible 'high' all day. Orders are being shouted at me one after another, and the radio crackles in my ear the whole time. I have to interpret the incoming traffic at top speed, and report my own movements and sightings. The gunfire and the engine noise beats on my head like a drum, all day long.

'When we stop at last, the silence feels incredible! But I have to report for the squadron commander's briefing straight away. Luckily my lads 'brew up' for me while I'm away. In a combat situation I expect absolute, instant obedience from them — our survival depends on it. But when we bivouac we can relax; my stripes don't stop us being good mates. It doesn't matter if you've got a million-dollar box of tricks to ride round in; if the men inside are no good, forget it.'

(Opposite) MG ammunition resupply for a Challenger crew from the Royal Hussars during 'CAT-87'.

THE LOADER

'. . . When the commander gives the fire order I select the round, and shove it into the breech fast as I can, and hit the 'ready to fire' safety button. I have to get my hands out of the way of the recoil pretty damn quick, and clear the breech right away, ready for the next round . . . I'm responsible for keeping an eye on the ammo stocks, too, and for stowing it when we get resupply. Manhandling 40 shells, and 20 boxes of MG belts, that's no picnic — but the guys help me out, of course . . .'

(Above) During 'CAT-85', a Belgian loader from the 2nd Lancers on radio watch.

THE TANK COMMANDER

'. . . In this job I'm responsible for a machine which costs a fortune, and for the three other lads. I direct the tank's movement by talking the driver through the terrain — he can't see much, stuck down there, especially when we're 'buttoned up' and he's using periscopes. I have to be a tactician to do that: we have to use the least fold in the ground to mask us — and sneaking 50 tons of steel along 'on its belly' is a knack that takes some learning. Like any other soldier I had to develop an eye for finding a good fire position, another to move to, and a fall-back position — and keep doing it, until it was instinctive.

(Right) Bundeswehr tank commander from PzBn. 134, 5 PzDiv. waits for orders on a rainy day.

THE FORCES ON THE GROUND

The Berlin Wall has fallen. The USSR intends to pull out of East Germany 2,700 tanks, and an armoured division each from both Czechoslovakia and Hungary. East Germany, Czechoslovakia and Poland have announced their intention to scrap, or convert for peaceful agricultural use, a total of some 1,450 older-model Soviet tanks. And yet, despite the facile arguments for almost total disarmament which are found in some Western publications, the imbalance in conventional forces between NATO and the Red Army remains as massively unfavourable as ever. The only weapons capable of balancing the account — medium and short range missiles — are in the process of being negotiated away.

A year ago the astonishing collapse of Russia's eastern European empire could not have been foreseen. Given the speed and confusion of political developments in the Soviet Union itself, is it impossible to believe that the West may one day find itself again facing up to a brutally reversed policy in Moscow? Even after all the promised cuts have been made, the Red Army will remain by far the most powerful force on the Continent. The figures speak for themselves.

Since 1976 every Soviet armoured division has received an 87% reinforcement in artillery and armoured fighting vehicles (AFVs). The number of actual tanks has remained constant at about 300 per division; but their quality has considerably improved. The T-80 cannot be much inferior to the American M1 Abrams. Since 1970 the Warsaw Pact has increased its tank strength by 22,000. In the same period only 7,300 new tanks have been delivered to the NATO regiments.

The Soviets have a total of 52 armoured divisions, 150 motorised divisions, and two large new formations of manoeuvre each equivalent to nearly four divisions. The Warsaw Pact has a total of 22,800 modern battle tanks (T-64, T-72, T-80); and 54,300 older second-line tanks (T-55, T-62), which are stored, and systematically up-rated. In total, the Warsaw Pact's potential battle tank strength thus approaches the incredible figure of 77,100. The less modern types are generally deployed in the southern and eastern military regions: the best face the West.

In the potential path of this armoured armada, NATO forces in Central Europe can deploy 15 armoured divisions and 12 mechanised divisions, with a total strength of 13,750 tanks. If the last reserves are scraped up, and all possible American, British, French, Spanish and Portuguese reinforcements are counted in, the grand total potentially available to NATO reaches just 22,000 tanks.

It is devoutly to be hoped that no reason ever arises again for an armed confrontation in Central Europe.

T-55 tank of the East German National People's Army during an exercise. Many thousands of these ageing tanks remain in second-line use with Soviet bloc armies. Despite the current detente and the announced withdrawals of Soviet troops from Eastern Europe, the numerical advantage remains at least three to one in favour of the USSR.

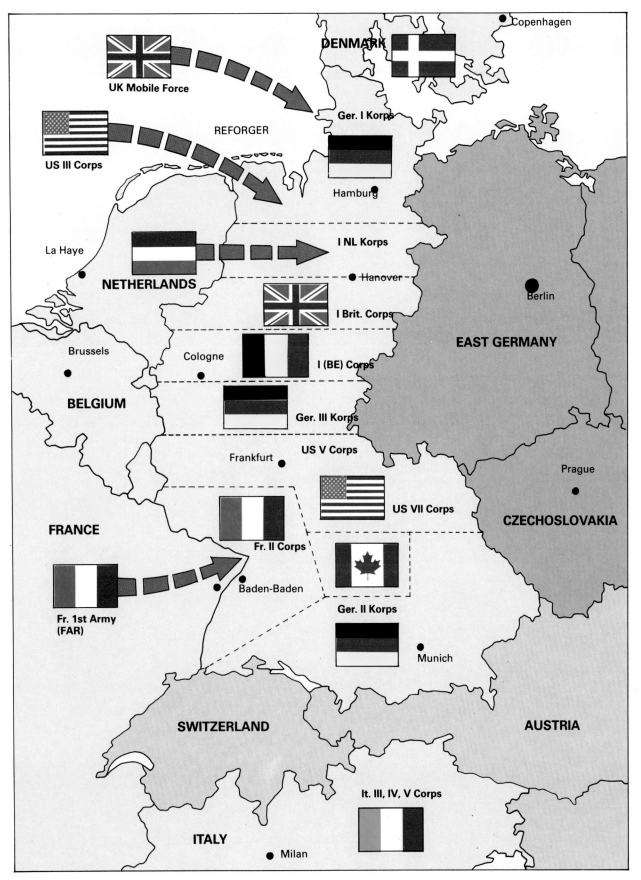

UK Mobile Force

US III Corps

REFORGER

DENMARK

Copenhagen

Ger. I Korps

Hamburg

La Haye

NETHERLANDS

I NL Korps

Hanover

EAST GERMANY

Berlin

I Brit. Corps

Brussels

Cologne

I (BE) Corps

BELGIUM

Ger. III Korps

US V Corps

Frankfurt

Prague

CZECHOSLOVAKIA

FRANCE

Fr. II Corps

US VII Corps

Fr. 1st Army
(FAR)

Baden-Baden

Ger. II Korps

Munich

SWITZERLAND

AUSTRIA

It. III, IV, V Corps

ITALY

Milan

DENMARK

Denmark possesses a strategic importance far beyond its small population and very limited defence budget. Adjacent to the sea-lanes of the Skagerrak and Kategat, the vital approaches to the Baltic, Denmark's tiny armed forces sit at the gates of the Soviet Navy's path from Leningrad and Kronstadt out into the Atlantic Ocean. A wartime scenario is easily imaginable. An attacking armoured force could push through Jutland, supported by airborne and sea-borne landing units which are in position, and which train regularly for intervention in the Baltic region.

The Danish army has 31,000 men, a third of them conscripts; wartime mobilisation would raise the figure to 48,000, plus 64,000 'territorials'. The Danes participate willingly in local defence exercises, though military service is generally unpopular. In any emergency the Danes would rely largely upon their allies. NATO's Mobile Brigade frequently exercises in this region, and West Germany's 6th Mechanised Division is tasked with defending its southern approaches.

Denmark has no large armoured formations. The army is deployed in five infantry brigades — three in Jutland to the west, and two in Seeland to the east — plus an independent battalion on the island of Bornholm. Each brigade has one tank battalion and two motorised infantry battalions. Each tank battalion has three tank companies and one of infantry mounted in M113 APCs. Each geographical division has a reconnaissance battalion with M41 tanks; and a reserve brigade also fields some 111 old Mk.3 Centurions. The theoretically available armour totals 120 Leopard 1 A3, 106 up-rated Mk.5/2 and 111 unmodernised Centurion, and 48 up-rated M41 A1 tanks.

(Below) M41 Walker Bulldog — not one of the up-rated batch — in service with the recce element of the Guard Hussars during the British exercise 'Eternal Triangle' in 1986.

(Opposite) Modernised Centurion of the Danish Guard, flaunting national colours from the antenna and the bison insignia of the Seeland Division.

ORDER OF BATTLE

Jutland Division
5th Reconnaissance Battalion (M41)
Jutland Dragoon Regiment (Leopard 1)

Seeland Division
3rd Reconnaissance Battalion (M41)
Guard Hussars Regiment (Centurion)

Bornholm Force
Company (M41)

Lurking in one of the rare
areas of cover on the great
northern European plain, a
Danish Centurion waits in
ambush for British troops
during 'Eternal Triangle 86'.
The Danes are the last
NATO army to retain this
classic tank, which saw
widespread combat in the
1950s and 1960s.

THE MODERNISED CENTURION
In 1962 the 4,423rd and last Centurion rolled off the
British Royal Ordnance Factory production lines.
Conceived as a counter to the *Tiger* late in the Second
World War, the long-developed Centurion series saw
world-wide service, and many victorious battles, in the
British and many other armies. Again, the Danes
decided to up-rate 106 of theirs. The 90mm gun was
replaced by the classic L-7 105mm, and a 12.7mm
(.50in.) machine gun was mounted on the turret. A
Swedish Ericson sighting system and Neodynium
YAG laser range-finder replaced the old sights. Thus
modernised, the Danish Centurion could serve on
until the end of the century. Some 111 of the old 20-
pdr. Centurions are retained by reserve units.

(Above) Exercise 'Bold Guard 87' on the Baltic coast: a modernised M41 lands from a Bundeswehr barge. Though elderly, the light M41 in its up-rated version is still a useful asset among the many islands of the Baltic seaboard.

THE MODERNISED M41 WALKER BULLDOG

An excellent light tank introduced in the 1950s and blooded in Korea and Vietnam, the M41 served for many years in NATO recce battalions. Rather than retire the ageing design altogether, the Danes decided to up-date it. This version, modernised by the Falck Schmidt company, has a larger turret fitted with a laser range-finder, infra-red projector and NBC equipment. The main armament remains the 76mm gun — the planned 90mm replacement was found too heavy by the US Army years ago — but now takes new APFSDS ammunition. The original engine has been replaced by a Cummins VTA-903T diesel developing 465hp.

GREAT BRITAIN

The cavalry arm of the British Army is divided into three organisations: the Household Cavalry, the Royal Armoured Corps, and the Yeomanry. The Household Cavalry comprises the two armoured regiments of the Guards — the Life Guards, and the Blues & Royals — both equipped with Scorpion and Scimitar CVRT ('combat vehicle, reconnaissance, tracked'). The Yeomanry is the armoured cavalry arm of the Territorial Army — the British equivalent of the US National Guard. Its two regiments, based in separated squadrons around the country, operate various light-armoured vehicles but not tracked gun-tanks.

The Royal Armoured Corps, with most of its 17 armoured regiments stationed in West Germany, represents the main weight of Britain's NATO contingent.

The British Army of the Rhine (BAOR) is by far the largest organisation of British combat units, and is committed to NATO. The 1st British Corps holds a sector stretching from Hanover to Kassel; its major formations are the 1st, 3rd and 4th Armoured Divisions; in time of emergency the corps would be reinforced by the 2nd Infantry Division from the UK. All British soldiers are volunteers, well-motivated and well-trained professionals. Their mission is simple: 1st and 4th Armoured Divisions would hold the front line, while 3rd Armoured Division, slightly to their rear, prepared a counter-attack. The 2nd Infantry Division would occupy the rear areas.

The composition of a British armoured division is complex. The combat units are grouped in three brigades (two, in the 3rd Armoured Division), whose composition varies according to mission. Some have two tank battalions and one mechanised infantry;

some, the reverse. 'Regiments' of the Royal Armoured Corps (tactically, of single battalion strength) have 57 tanks if equipped with Chieftains, and 43 if they have received the progressively introduced Challenger. The Challenger squadron (company) has four troops (platoons) of three tanks each, and three tanks in the HQ troop. Each regiment also has a reconnaissance troop of eight Scorpion CVRT. (Similar recce platoons serve with the battalions of mechanised infantry.)

So far a total of some 380 Challengers have been delivered to seven tank regiments; the rest are still equipped with some of the 500 Chieftains still in service, largely in the latest Mk.15 version. The British tank force in West Germany is neither equipped nor configured for sweeping advances or deep penetrations of enemy terrain; it is a massive weapon of defence and counter-attack, long trained over every mile of the ground it would have to defend in an emergency.

(Below) Exercise 'White Rhino 89': Challengers of the Royal Scots Dragoon Guards, their turrets traversed to '3 o'clock', roll across West Germany.

(Opposite) David and Goliath: a Scimitar of the regimental recce troop and a Challenger MBT of the Royal Hussars in a Saxon village during 'Eternal Triangle 86'.

BRITISH ARMOURED REGIMENTS

Since the 1920s numerous regimental amalgamations
have resulted in the double numbering of many
cavalry regiments.

Household Cavalry	5th Royal Inniskilling Dragoon Guards
	Queen's Own Hussars
Life Guards	Queen's Royal Irish Hussars
Blues & Royals	9th/12th Royal Lancers
	Royal Hussars
	13th/18th Royal Hussars
Royal Armoured Corps	14th/20th King's Hussars
	15th/19th King's Royal Hussars
1st Queen's Royal Dragoon Guards	16th/5th Queen's Royal Lancers (CVRT)
Royal Scots Dragoon Guards	17th/21st Lancers
4th/7th Royal Dragoon Guards	1st,2nd,3rd & 4th Royal Tank Regiment.

CHIEFTAIN —
PONDEROUS POWER

(Below) Chieftain Mk.9 of the 17th/21st Lancers waits for American M1s during exercise 'Trutziche Sachsen 85'. The 17th/21st are a good example of regimental tradition; their black beret bears the death's-head badge dating from the raising of the unit by the officer who brought the news of Gen. Wolfe's death at Quebec in 1759. (Bottom) Mk. 9 of the Royal Scots Dragoon Guards — the 'Scots Greys', of Waterloo legend — firing on the move during 'CAT-85'. The regiment has since re-equipped with Challenger.

Adopted by the British Army in May 1963 after four years of prototype trials, the Chieftain was built by the Royal Ordnance Factory at Leeds and by Vickers. A total of 900 of various versions have been delivered. Over the past decade about half BAOR's tank strength has been replaced by the newer Challenger, but some 500 Chieftains remain in service. Small numbers have been exported to the Middle East.

For about 15 years the Chieftain was the West's hardest hitting tank. Its unique 120mm L-11 A5 gun and — in their day — state-of-the-art fire controls gave it massive firepower and deadly accuracy. Its designers had chosen to emphasise firepower and protection rather than manoeuvrability; its armour was very impressive, but it lacked the speed and mobility of contemporary French and German tanks. There were reliability problems with the engines of early marks,

later solved. In a basically defensive weapon this was a tolerable mix of characteristics; and even today, in its Mk.15 version with added 'Stillbrew' armour (classified, but probably comparable to Chobham armour in conception), it remains a formidable tank well adapted to British tactical doctrine. Its leading position in the firepower competition has now been lost to the Leopard 2 and Abrams, however.

(Below) The massive bulk of a Chieftain Mk. 15 — the last of the series, protected with additional 'Stillbrew' armour; here the Queen's Own Hussars wait to go into action during 'White Rhino 89'.

(Above) Brand new Challenger of the Royal Hussars at the start of a firing run during the 'CAT-87' competitions.

CHALLENGER —
BORN FOR THE EAST

(Below) The lieutenant-colonel commanding, Royal Hussars, directs his Challengers during 'Eternal Triangle 86'. The regimental beret bears a badge first adopted by England's Prince of Wales as a mark of respect for a gallant fallen enemy at Crécy in 1346.

In 1977 rising costs finally caused the cancellation of 'MBT-80', a joint British-German project; this left Britain with only a vague plan for a tank for the 1980s. However, at that time a tank ordered for the Imperial Iranian army was in full development in Britain — 'Shir 2'. This was in fact an up-dated development of the Chieftain with the latest Chobham armour.

The Iranian revolution and the fall of the Shah put an effective stop to the Shir 2 programme. The British government came to the rescue of the Royal Ordnance Factory, ordering for British use the 237 Shir 2 tanks already in production, with modifications to fit them for European service. The MBT-80 was definitively abandoned, and the new tank was christened Challenger. In later years supplementary orders for another 64 and 76 examples were placed, permitting the re-equipment of seven tank regiments in all.

The main armament is again the 120mm L-11 A5 gun, but there have been some problems with the sophisticated fire controls. The system of gun loading is also potentially slower than desirable, involving the separate loading of projectile and self-consuming case, though this system has the advantage of not cluttering the turret with large empty shell cases. The mobility of the Challenger is much improved over the Chieftain, and it has a top speed of 60km/h (38 mph). The Chobham armour gives the tank excellent protection against current types of projectile. (An additional design feature which is greatly appreciated by the crews is an on-board heater for brewing tea!)

The Challenger 2 project, featuring an improved turret and fire controls, is currently at the development stage, but a question-mark hangs over its future given the latest developments in the Soviet bloc.

(Opposite) Ancient and modern: a Challenger of 2nd Royal Tank Regiment passes the foot of one of the bastions dominating the River Weser — which in olden times must have brooded over the passing of many armoured warriors.

SCORPION AND SCIMITAR CVRT

Employed for reconnaissance, these two versions of one design series are real little jewels — but although they look like 'mini-tanks', they are more realistically thought of as a kind of big, armoured, turreted jeep, as their armour only gives protection from the lighter calibres of ammunition. Their engine is a Jaguar J-60, similar to the powerplant of the big Jaguar sports cars; and this, coupled with their light weight, gives an astonishing theoretical top road speed of more than 60 mph (96km/h). Their lightness is achieved by the use of aluminium armour; it gives a ground pressure of only .35kg (.77lb) per square inch, giving excellent flotation on the softest ground. It also allows the CVRT to be carried as a slung load under RAF Chinook helicopters, or — two at a time — to be stowed inside the C-130 Hercules.

The small turret mounts a long automatic 30mm Rarden cannon in the Scimitar; this takes three-round clips, and if two are coupled the gun can fire six-round bursts. Special APSE ('armour piercing special effect') ammunition is supplied, which can penetrate a light-armoured vehicle and cause spectacular damage inside. The Scorpion version mounts a 76mm gun, whose usual load is the HESH ('high explosive squash head') round.

(Above) The CVRT series serves in the reconnaissance troops of British mechanised infantry battalions. Here a Scimitar of the Royal Irish Rangers makes use of its high top speed along a German road. (Below) A detachment from the 9th/12th Royal Lancers halt under cover.

In 1982 two troops from B Squadron, Blues & Royals took four Scorpions, four Scimitars and a Samson recovery vehicle to the Falklands during Operation 'Corporate'. Although the Argentine Panhard armoured cars never left the safety of Port Stanley to give fight, the CVRTs — able to operate over the very boggy terrain without much difficulty — proved useful as 'bunker-busters' in support of infantry attacks.

Britain has some 2,000 CVRTs in service, and Belgium has taken delivery of 700.

DESCENDANTS OF 'HOBART'S FUNNIES'

The reliable old Centurion still serves in one capacity in the British army: as the chassis for various specialised 'Assault Vehicles, Royal Engineers'. The tradition established by Gen. Hobart's 79th Armd. Div. in 1944-45, when this entire division of special 'funnies' mounted on Sherman and Churchill tank chassis greatly contributed to the Allied advance in NW Europe, is recalled today in the 'Centurion funnies' of the Royal Engineers' 32 Armoured Engineer Regiment.

(Above and right) Centurions equipped with obstacle-crossing fascine, dozer-blade, and short 165mm 'bunker-busting' gun.

In action — Challengers of the Royal Scots Dragoon Guards during exercise 'White Rhino 89'.

THE NETHERLANDS

Long hair and unionised conscripts have not always attracted good publicity; but the Dutch army's leadership cadre is very professional, logistics are sound, and equipment is relatively modern. The bulk of the Dutch land forces are grouped in 1st Corps, which forms part of NORTHAG, the major NATO command which defends Central Europe's northern front. In time of war 1st Corps would advance into West Germany and take up position between Hamburg and Hanover facing the Soviet 2nd Guards Army. Their mission is starkly simple: to try to prevent the Warsaw Pact forces breaking through on to the great billiard-table of the northern European plain — a 480km (300 mile) corridor pointing at the Dutch ports, vital for NATO reinforcement and supply.

In peacetime 1st Corps has a strength of 35,000 men, of whom 25,000 are conscripts; in wartime another 40,000 reservists would be recalled to the colours.

The Dutch 1st Corps has no armoured divisions *per se*, but three mechanised divisions: the 1st and 4th (active) and the 5th (reserve). Each has one armoured and two mechanised infantry brigades. The armoured brigades each have two tank battalions, of three squadrons each, and one mechanised battalion. As in nearly all NATO armies, the composition of mechanised brigades is reversed — two mechanised infantry battalions and one tank battalion.

(Opposite, top and bottom) Dutchmen in France: Leopard 1 tanks of the Netherlands' 13th Armd. Bde. visit the Mourmelon ranges during autumn 1989. The Leopard 1 AV (V for Verbeterd, 'improved') is an A1 with new Phillips fire controls and added spaced armour.

(Above) Leopard 2s of Pantserbataljon 43 in Germany, 1987, during the huge exercise 'Certain Strike'.

(Right) Behind his MAG superstructure gun, a Dutch tank commander waits for an ARV — the yellow flag means 'breakdown'.

Movement would be the great problem for the Dutch armour. Currently only the 41st Brigade is stationed permanently in West Germany; the other units of 1st Corps would face a long march to reach their battle stations in any emergency.

The Dutch have around 1,000 tanks: 468 Leopard 1 (which are going to be up-dated) and 445 Leopard 2. In reserve units a total of 126 old AMX-13s are still in use, though not all are operational.

ORDER OF BATTLE

1st Division
11th Mechanised Infantry Brigade
12th Mechanised Infantry Brigade
13th Armoured Brigade

4th Division
41st Armoured Brigade
42nd Mechanised Infantry Brigade
43rd Mechanised Infantry Brigade

5th (Reserve) Division
51st Armoured Brigade
52nd Mechanised Infantry Brigade
53rd Mechanised Infantry Brigade

Armoured column from the Dutch 41st Armoured Brigade await the word to attack the US '1st Cav', brought over from the United States for exercise 'Reforger 87'.

BELGIUM

For a country of its limited size and population Belgium has considerable military assets. Without being warmongers, the Belgians have earned a good military reputation. Unfortunately, the country's economic situation seriously limits the current defence budget, and troops are relatively thin on the ground. The 1st (BE) Corps, in which the main operational units are grouped, is committed to NORTHAG in time of war. Sixty per cent of the corps' effectives are stationed in West Germany, with headquarters near Cologne. The defensive sector assigned to the Belgian corps is a 100km (62 mile) zone between Kassel and Aix-la-Chappelle. The 1st (BE) Corps comprises two mechanised divisions, each of two brigades; in time of emergency two more brigades would be activated. Each mechanised infantry brigade has one battalion of Leopard tanks, and there are two in the armoured brigade.

Each tank battalion comprises three squadrons each of four platoons each of three tanks, plus the squadron commander's tank. A total of 334 Leopard 1 tanks are in service, and will not be replaced before the year 2000. They are already fitted with the excellent SABCA fire controls; and a modernisation package to bring fire controls and armour up to A1 standard is planned.

The Belgian cavalry has proud traditions stretching back centuries to Belgian dragoons in Austrian service. These traditions are maintained, and among NATO tankmen Belgian crews enjoy a high reputation: they nearly always score highly in the Canadian Army Trophy firing competitions, even against more modern tanks.

ORDER OF BATTLE

1st Division (HQ Verviers, Belgium)

1st Mechanised Brigade (Leopoldburg)
7th Mech. Bde. (Marche-le-Famene)

16th Division (HQ Neheim, W.Germany)

4th Mech.Bde. (Soest)
17th Armd.Bde. (Siegen)

(Right) Belgian Leopard 1 Al of the 2nd *Jageers te Paard* (the Flemish title for *Chasseurs à cheval*, since this is a Flemish-speaking unit). In the near future Belgian tankers should benefit from a modernisation package (and a new camouflage scheme) for their Leopard 1s.

(Below) Leopard 1 Al of Belgium's 1st Lancers in action during 'Certain Strike 87'; note the blank-firing system above the barrel.

(Above) Scorpion and Scimitar recce vehicles of the Belgian 4th Chasseurs; the recce platoons of Belgium's Reconnaissance Command each have two of each version of the CVRT series.

SCORPION AND SCIMITAR

The Belgians also maintain a major command for their reconnaissance units, COM RECCE, based at Arolsen in Germany. Comprising two battalions of Leopards and two of CVRT Scorpion and Scimitar light armoured vehicles, its mission is to reconnoitre the movements of the potential enemy, in this case the Soviet 3rd Shock Army. The 133 Scorpions and 153 Scimitars are divided between squadrons of *Chasseurs à Cheval* and the recce platoons of the Leopard units. (The crack Para-Commandos also have a recce squadron of these fast AFVs.)

JAGDPANZERKANONE

The Belgians are the last NATO army to keep in service a turretless 'tank destroyer' armed with a cannon, in the classic Second World War mould: the 90mm JPK ('*Jagdpanzerkanone*') equips the AT companies of eight infantry battalions, ten per company. (The *Bundeswehr* retains this German vehicle but with the gun replaced by AT missiles.) This low-profile AFV, with modernised fire controls, could still prove valuable in defensive fighting.

(Left and opposite) The image recalls World War II — JPK tank destroyers of Belgium's 'Liberation' Battalion on the Frankfurt-Kassel highway during exercise 'Golden Crow'.

WEST GERMANY

(Above) Panzerbataillon 121 pushes on across Bavaria during the wide-ranging exercise 'Tough Sparrow', which pitted the Panzerwaffe against France's Rapid Action Force.

If Germany was not the first nation to field tanks, it remains historically the great expert in the handling of armoured forces. The *Panzers* of the 1940-1941 *Blitzkrieg* — supple, manoeuvrable, and perfectly balanced in divisional organisation — made rings around enemies who were often numerically stronger, and sometimes technically more modern. Even during the last years of the war the dwindling *Panzerwaffe* more than held its own in anything approaching an equal contest.

Today's *Bundeswehr* is the most important conventional force in Western Europe, and its armoured units represent the lion's share of that force. In any conventional war the 12 *Panzer* and *Panzergrenadier* divisions would be NATO's armoured shield.

The Federal German army fields three large army corps, plus the 6th PzGren.Div. which has the task of defending Schleswig Holstein. Germany has 17 armoured and 15 *Panzergrenadier* (mechanised) brigades. Generally, the military organisation follows the 'triangular' doctrine: the division has three combat brigades, the brigade three battalions, the battalion

three companies, the company three platoons — though the platoon has four tanks, and the company commander a 13th tank. The armoured division has one mechanised and two armoured brigades: the mechanised division, the reverse. The mechanised brigade differs in having three mechanised battalions and a single armoured battalion.

Quality matches quantity, with some 1,800 Leopard 2 and 2,437 Leopard 1 tanks. The Leopard 2 equips the battalions in the armoured brigades, the older model the battalions incorporated in the mechanised brigades.

The West German territorial defence forces include some 20 reserve tank battalions equipped with older Leopard 1s, and with M48 Pattons up-gunned with 105mm tubes.

The historically high reputation of German tank forces is confirmed by their tactical success in NATO manoeuvres. To see a *Panzerbrigade* in action is a fascinating sight; each company seems to maintain its place in an apparently rigid matrix — yet, almost always, there will be a battalion which finds the decisi-

Leopard 2 platoon from Panzerbataillon 364, 12 Panzerdivision regroup after an American attack during exercise 'Certain Challenge' in 1988.

vely weak point in the enemy's defence, and exploits it. The lively morale of the *Panzerwaffe* is particularly noticeable in an army not given to dramatic gesture; and one visit to the 'honour room' of a tank battalion confirms that the great traditions of the German tank arm are not forgotten.

ORDER OF BATTLE

I Corps:
1st Panzerdivision
1st PzGren.Bde., 2nd & 3rd Pz.Bdes.
3rd Panzerdivision
7th PzGren.Bde., 8th Pz.Bde., 9th Pz.Bde. 'Panzerlehr'
6th Panzergrenadierdivision
16th & 17th PzGren.Bde., 18th Pz.Bde., 51st Heimatshutz Bde.

7th Panzerdivision
19th PzGren.Bde., 20th & 21st Pz.Bdes.
11th Panzergrenadier Division
31st & 32nd PzGren.Bdes., 33rd Pz.Bde.
II Corps:
4th Panzergrenadier Division
10th & 11th PzGren.Bdes., 12th Pz.Bde.
10th Panzerdivision
28th & 29th Pz.Bdes., 30th PzGren.Bde.

1st Mountain Division
22nd PzGren.Bde., 23rd Mtn.Bde., 24th Pz.Bde.
III Corps:
5th Panzerdivision
14th & 15th Pz.Bdes., 13th PzGren.Bde.
12th Panzerdivision
34th & 36th Pz.Bdes., 35th PzGren.Bde.
2nd Panzergrenadier Division
4th & 5th PzGren.Bdes., 6th Pz.Bde.

LEOPARD 1 — NATO'S WARHORSE

Like the AMX-30, the Leopard 1 should have had its origin in a joint Franco-German project. In the event, for political as much as technical reasons, the project was not pursued; and Germany turned to the Munich firm of Krauss-Maffei, which had been picked to produce the hull of the joint project. A new turret was designed; and the result was the Leopard, Germany's first post-war tank. Several NATO countries — and also Australia — ordered this excellent design.

Over the course of time a continual process of development has changed the latest models radically from the original tank. Only the basic hull remains unchanged. In the Leopard 1 the designers went for mobility over armour protection: with a ten-cylinder, 830hp MTU engine the 40-ton Leopard 1 achieved a top speed of 65kmh. — astonishing by contrast with, say, the massive Chieftain. The classic L-7 A3 gun was selected; and today some Leopard 1s have been retrospectively fitted with the Belgian SABCA fire controls, giving a 99% probability of hitting the target.

The standard NATO tank for many years, the Leopard 1 will remain in service with several armies until the year 2000.

Variants:

Leopard 1 A1 Fitted with a thermal sleeve for the cannon and an additional armour package on the turret and gun.

Leopard 1 A2 New supporting sleeve for the gun barrel, improved steel turret protection, improved NBC system, passive image intensification vision system for commander and driver.

Leopard 1 A3 Entirely redesigned turret with large rear bustle.

Leopard 1 A4 Externally similar to the A3, but with improved fire controls with stabilised panoramic periscope for the commander; gunner's controls coupled to stereoscopic range-finder, and armament stabilised by ballistic computer.

(Right) On its way to relieve Belgian units during 'Certain Strike 87', this Leopard 1 A3 of PzBn. 14, 1 PzDiv. shows off the additional armour bolted to its turret as part of the up-rating programme.

(Left) Spattered with mud and displaying its red cross exercise markings, a Leopard 1 A3 from PzBn. 104 waits for German and French paratroopers during exercise 'Kolibri 87'.

(Right) The traditional insignia of the Panzerwaffe — the iron fist of the medieval hero Götz von Berlichingen — painted on the turret of a Leopard 1 A4 from PzBn. 134, seen here during winter training at Graffenswohr.

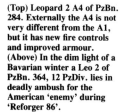

LEOPARD 2 — ODIN'S FIRE

(Top) Leopard 2 A4 of PzBn. 284. Externally the A4 is not very different from the A1, but it has new fire controls and improved armour.
(Above) In the dim light of a Bavarian winter a Leo 2 of PzBn. 364, 12 PzDiv. lies in deadly ambush for the American 'enemy' during 'Reforger 86'.

When the Leopard 1 was in full production at the end of the 1960s the Porsche company was commissioned to produce a study for a new MBT. At the same time West Germany and the USA decided to co-operate in designing a tank for the end of the century. A common prototype, designated MBT-70, was built; but it was soon dismissed as too expensive, and each country turned back on its national resources for a new tank.

Using their experience with the engine, transmission, and various other assemblies planned for the MBT-70, the Germans made 16 prototypes and 17 turrets of a new tank which would become the Leopard 2. After many trials in both the USA and West Germany it was adopted for the *Bundeswehr*, with a smooth-bore 120mm Rheinmetall cannon. Of 1,800 ordered 810 were built by Krupp and 990 by Krauss-

Maffei. In 1987 another 250 were ordered, partly for the 10th Pz Div., whose Leopard 1 A3 tanks were earmarked for sale to Turkey.

In NATO, the Dutch picked the Leopard 2 to replace their Centurions and some of their AMX-13s; and, after a punishing series of competitive trials with the M1 Abrams, the Leopard was selected for licence production by the Swiss.

For the tankman, the Leopard 2 is a dream. Powerful and fast despite its 55 tons, it matches the protection of Chobham armour with the firepower of the 120mm gun. Its ammunition capacity of 42 rounds (20 less than its predecessor) is off-set by the penetrative power of the 120mm and the very sophisticated fire controls: every shell will count. The gun fires HEAT-MPT rounds, suitable for all battlefield targets, and

APFSDS-T rounds, deadly to all known tanks; self-consuming cases prevent the cluttering of the fighting compartment in action.

As in the Leopard 1, the commander has his own 'override' aiming controls, aiming telescope, and battlefield surveillance camera. The gunner has stabilised EMES 15 fire controls, comprising a laser rangefinder and a thermal imager. The crew is protected by a comprehensive NBC system, and an automatic fire-extinguishing system. The multi-fuel engine develops 1,500hp, giving even this 55-ton monster a power to weight ratio of 27hp/t (the Leopard 1 boasted 20hp/t) and the extraordinary top speed of 72km/h (44mph).

Arguably the best tank currently in unit service, the Leopard 2 is an incredibly destructive and highly manoeuvrable weapon — 'Odin's Fire' returned to earth.

Massive and threatening power: a Leopard 2 from Panzerbataillon 124, 4 Panzergrenadierdivision, photographed during exercise 'Buntes Faunlein'.

CANADA

(Above) Leopards of the
Royal Canadian Dragoons
support the movement of
another troop of their
squadron during exercise
'Buntes Faunlein', 1986. The
highly-trained RCDs take
part in many manoeuvres in
southern Germany.

Officially, Canada has no 'Army'; in 1968 all three armed services were merged into the 'Canadian Forces', within which the land force is termed 'Mobile Command'. It is 18,000 strong, all-volunteer, and operationally divided into three Brigade Groups and the Special Service Group. 4th Brigade Group is based in West Germany under CENTAG and 5th Bde.Gp., in Canada, is earmarked for NATO reinforcement in time of emergency — formerly, to northern Norway, but currently to Germany.

Canada built 114 Leopard 1 A3C tanks under licence, and the greater part serve in Germany with the Royal Canadian Dragoons. This is the armoured battalion of 4th Bde.Gp., which also fields two mechanised infantry battalions and support units. The armoured battalion has three 12-tank squadrons plus reconnaissance and supply companies.

The 'RCDs' are a mixed Anglo/French-speaking unit, whose well-trained regular crews enjoy a high reputation. Despite the small size of Canada's tank force, it instituted the famous Canadian Army Trophy — the 'CAT' takes place every two years, and is NATO's premier competition for tank skills.

(Right) Three different
configurations of the
Leopard 1 A3C of the RCDs.
Each squadron has two tanks
fitted with dozer-blades.

UNITED STATES OF AMERICA

With 12,130 tanks the USA ranks second only to the Soviet Union as the greatest armoured power in the world. Many of this total are, of course, second-line vehicles — M48 and M60 A1 Pattons — serving with the National Guard. But the recent introduction of the M1 Abrams to replace the M60 A3 in first-line units gives the US tank force a world-beater.

The bulk of America's tank force is in West Germany; the only major formations on home station are the 2nd Armored Division and 1st Cavalry Division, both at Fort Hood, Texas.

American land forces in Germany (USAREUR), headquartered at Frankfurt, comprise the V and VII Army Corps. Each corps has one armoured division — the 3rd and 1st respectively. An additional independent brigade, administratively linked to the 2nd Armd. Div., is based at Garlstedt in north Germany.

The powerful US armoured divisional organisation includes six tank and four mechanised battalions. The mechanised divisions each have five tank battalions; three such formations serve in Germany. The arrival of the M1 Abrams led to the reorganisation of the tank battalion, previously 54 M60s in three companies; now 56 M1s are divided between four companies, the HQ company having a further two. Each company has

THE US ARMORED CORPS

In the USA:	National Guard
I Corps	49th & 50th Armd.Divs.
9th Inf.Div. (Experimental)	30th, 31st, 149th, 155th Sep. Armd.Bd
III Corps	107th, 116th, 163rd, 278th Armd.Cav.
1st Inf.Div. (Mechanised)	
1st Cavalry Div.	In West Germany:
2nd Armored Div.	*V Corps*
4th Inf.Div. (Mech.)	11th Armd.Cav.Regt.
5th Inf.Div. (Mech.)	3rd Armd. Div.
24th Inf.Div. (Mech.)	8th Inf.Div. (Mech.)

three platoons of four tanks, and two in the company HQ platoon.

The 'tankers' of the M1 battalions are the spearhead of US Army power in Europe; they give the impression of being highly competent and motivated by comparison with some other units, are conscious of their élite position, and are proud of their superb machines. In recent NATO competitions the M1 and the *Bundeswehr* Leopard 2 have hotly disputed the top prizes; and when a US tanker, beer in hand, loudly declared during a CAT meeting 'I'm the best tanker in the world, in the best tank!', it would have been a bold man who tried to prove him wrong.

(Below) An officer of the 1st Cavalry Division wearing the traditional black Stetson.

VII Corps
2nd Armd.Cav.Regt.
1st Armd.Div.
3rd Inf.Div. (Mech.)
1st Inf.Div. (Mech.)

In South Korea:
2nd Inf.Div. (Mech.)

M60 A3 of 1/81st Armor making a fast turn during exercise 'Certain Sentinel 86'. This is one of the battalions of the 1st Armored Division, 'Old Ironsides', permanently based in Germany.

M60 —
THE LAST PATTON

(Below) M60 of 12th Cavalry, 3rd Armored Division photographed in a Bavarian village during 'Certain Challenge'. Each armoured division has an Armd. Cav. regiment for reconnaissance work.

In 1956 the US Army issued a requirement for a new tank based on the successful M48. Three M48s were modified and fitted with the latest equipment under the designation M48 A2 E1; after tests and further modifications they were rebaptised XM60, and gave birth to a new series of Patton tanks. The first became operational in 1962, its origins still traceable to the M26 Pershing of 1944 which had been planned as a counter to the terrible German *Tiger*.

The latest version, M60 A3, with laser range-finder and sophisticated fire controls, is beyond doubt one of the most impressive tanks in the world: in fact, one's first close encounter with any Patton puts one in mind of a cathedral on tracks! The great height of this basically 1940s design is its major drawback — today's generation of tanks have become much lower and more streamlined, and thus much harder to see, hit, and disable.

For 20 years the M60 was the mount of the US Armored Corps, and it still serves in great numbers with the second-line units of the National Guard and with US-allied armies. It is strong, reliable, without major mechanical quirks, and easy to maintain; and although gun-armed M60s did not fight in Vietnam, it has a good reputation among Israeli tankers, who have crewed it under the hardest combat conditions. It has better protection than the Leopard 1 or the AMX-30. The A3 variant has a new RISE AVDs 1790 engine, new tracks, a new anti-distortion barrel sleeve, new stabilisers, and new fire controls. A bull-dozer blade or a minesweeping attachment can both be fitted. The A2 version, which mounted a massive 152mm gun capable of firing conventional ammunition or Shillelagh missiles, was abandoned on the grounds of excessive complexity. Curiously, the US Marine Corps has never used the A3 — the 'Leather-necks' retain the older A1 in their landing units.

(Below) Rendered even more than usually impressive by its dozer-blade, this massive M60 A3 of 64th Armor, 1st Armd. Div. takes part in exercise 'Buntes Faunlein' with German sappers: note 'Fuchs' all-terrain vehicle in the background.

Following the abandonment of the joint German-American MBT-70 project, the US Army adopted — after lengthy competitive trials of different prototypes — a Chrysler design for a new main battle tank to take the US Armored Corps into the 21st century. In 1978 pre-series construction was completed under the designation XM1. Initial production began late in 1979, the first batch being delivered in 1981. The M1 was named 'Abrams' after Gen.Creighton Abrams, Second World War commander of the crack 37th Tank Bn., 4th Armored Division.

The Abrams had to suffer a great deal of largely ill-informed criticism at this early stage. It was a revolutionary design, and inevitably there were bugs to be ironed out, but some of the attacks launched by press and politicians were breathtakingly silly. Luckily, the judgement of professional tank soldiers prevailed.

The M1 is the first tank in the world to be powered by a diesel turbine engine. This is thirsty, but gives extraordinary acceleration (0-20mph in six seconds) and a top road speed of 45mph — which makes the M1 an elusive battlefield target. The AGT-1500 turbine is much easier to service and replace than more conventional engines: the whole assembly can be lifted out

A relaxed M1 crew of the 2nd Armd. Cav. Regt. wait for movement orders. This unit is tasked with keeping watch on the Czechoslovak frontier.

(Opposite) Who else but the evilly grinning Garfield should adorn the turret of this M1 from 3/64th Armor taking part in the 'CAT-85' competition? The sophisticated fire controls of the Abrams allow it to 'eat up' targets like lasagne, after all . . .

M1 ABRAMS — REVOLUTIONARY THOROUGHBRED

(Right) Brand new M1 A1 of 1/67th Armor, 3rd Armd. Div. 'Spearhead', showing off the acceleration which is one of the M1's most striking capabilities.

and replaced in an hour, an enormous advantage. In theory the engine should last 12,500 miles. Track mileage is more limited, and averages 850 miles.

The silhouette of the Abrams is very low; combined with Chobham armour and an automatic fire-suppression system, this makes it hard to hit, harder to penetrate, and harder still to destroy. The large and relatively comfortable fighting compartment is designed with crew safety in mind; ammunition storage bins are arranged so that any explosion is channelled outwards. There is even an automatic guard which comes between the breech and the loader to prevent recoil injuries.

Initially rather under-gunned with the M68 cannon (the US version of the 105mm British L-7), the Abrams can claim the compensatory high performance of new tungsten carbide and depleted uranium APFSDS shells. The improved M1 A1 has the 120mm Rheinmetall gun of the Leopard 2. Fire controls are 'state-of-the-art'; and the Abrams have proved itself a truly revolutionary tank, triumphing in NATO manoeuvres and competitions. Some British authorities argue that Britain should acquire the M1 'off the shelf' instead of developing Challenger 2.

FRANCE

In time of war France would activate the 1st Army, the organisation comprising the greater part of her land forces. It is today tasked with planning and preparing for the engagement of French forces in Central Europe. The major components of those land forces are the Armoured Mechanised Corps and the Rapid Action Force. Their mission would be to contain any aggressor while the government decided on an appropriate response. In such an emergency it is most likely that French forces would be committed to NATO: while not part of the NATO integrated military command in peacetime, the French forces maintain close links with the alliance, and bi-lateral mutual defence agreements.

Apart from organic units, the 1st Army consists of three army corps which represent the bulk of France's conventional defence assets. The principal weapon of offence is the armoured division of some 150 AMX-30 tanks. France's armoured formations are disposed as follows:

1st Corps (HQ Metz)
7th Armoured Division, 15th Infantry Division. Wartime reinforcements would include the 12th and 14th Light Armoured Divisions, which in peacetime are training formations based normally at Saumur and Montpellier respectively.

2nd Corps/'French Forces in Germany' (HQ Baden-Baden)
1st, 3rd and 5th Armoured Divisions. This is the spearhead of 1st Army, and is equipped almost entirely with up-rated AMX-30 B2 tanks.

3rd Corps (HQ Lille)
2nd and 10th Armoured Divisions, 8th Infantry Division.

According to its category and mission a French armoured division comprises two or three tank regiments, a mechanised infantry regiment with AMX-10 P armoured personnel carriers, a motorised infantry regiment with VAB wheeled armoured personnel carriers, and divisional support units. Depending upon whether it belongs to a division with two or three tank regiments, a regiment fields either 70 or 52 AMX-30s. Within each mechanised infantry regiment there is also a company of tanks. The tank company/squadron has 17 AMX-30s in four platoons of four tanks plus the command tank. Total armoured fighting vehicles in service number some 3,000, of which nearly 1,500 are AMX-30 tanks. This impressive force is handicapped, however, by the increasing age of the AMX-30.

The Armoured Mechanised Corps could be reinforced in Central Europe by the Rapid Action Force, which is theoretically ready to mount a counter-attack at 24 hours notice. This light mobile organisation has no MBTs, but its heavy wheeled armoured cars represent a useful striking force. The roughly 72 AMX-10 RC and 100 ERC-90 Sagaie vehicles, mounting heavy cannon, are deployed among the Rapid Action Force's Spahi, Parachute, Foreign Legion, Marine and Alpine units, which are almost entirely composed of volunteer professionals, in contrast to the largely conscript bulk of the army. Many of these highly-trained and motivated units have tested their abilities on active service, sometimes under fire, in France's former African colonies.

French armoured regiments:
With AMX-10 RC: 6th Light Armoured Division (1st Foreign Cavalry Regiment, 1st Spahis). Committed to Rapid Action Force.
Plus: a reconnaissance regiment in each of the three army corps — 2nd, 3rd, and 8th Hussars — and in the 8th and 15th Infantry Divisions — 5th and 7th Chasseurs.
With ERC-90 Sagaie: Recce squadrons of the other Rapid Action Force divisions: 9th Marine Division (1st Para-Hussars, 1st Marine Inf.Regt., Moroccan Colonial Inf.Regt.); 27th Alpine Division (4th Chasseurs).

French armoured regiments with AMX-30:

1st Armoured Division
1st Cuirassiers, 6th Dragoons

2nd Armoured Division
6th Cuirassiers, 501st Combat Tanks,
2nd Dragoons

3rd Armoured Division
3rd Cuirassiers, 12th Cuirassiers

5th Armoured Division
2nd, 4th and 5th Cuirassiers

7th Armoured Division
1st Dragoons, 5th Dragoons, 3rd Chasseurs

10th Armoured Division
2nd Chasseurs, 4th Dragoons,
503rd Combat Tanks

12th Light Armoured Division
507th Combat Tank Regiment

14th Light Armoured Division
11th Cuirassiers

59

AMX-30

Conceived in the late 1950s, the AMX-30 is still the backbone of France's armoured corps. During the planning process it was envisaged that France and West Germany would produce jointly a common MBT for the 1960s, the Germans building the hull and the French the turret. As so often, political considerations interfered with the project when it was already under way; and France was left with an advanced turret design, but no hull. It was necessary to improvise with some urgency; and the resulting French hull

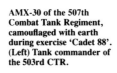

AMX-30 of the 507th Combat Tank Regiment, camouflaged with earth during exercise 'Cadet 88'. (Left) Tank commander of the 503rd CTR.

was rushed into service in a technically immature state, early series tanks being plagued by gearbox and transmission problems. These were solved in the AMX-30 B2 version, which now equips the great majority of armoured units. Even so, the AMX-30 B2 remains a 'first generation' tank retrospectively modernised, and is generally comparable to the Leopard 1 A3.

A total of 501 AMX-30 B2 have been built, and 1,657 AMX-30 B will have been up-rated to B2 standard by the time the last deliveries are made in 1993. The B2 will serve on until the end of the century, its useful life extended by the fitting of COTAC fire controls, an LLLTV camera permitting night operations, and a new transmission. The 105mm gun fires a French APFSDS round capable of penetrating 150mm of armour at an angle of 60° at 5,000 metres.

(Below) AMX-30 B2 under a stormy sky. It serves with the 4th Dragoons who, with the 503rd Combat Tanks, will have the honour of forming the first of the planned 80-tank regiments to receive the advanced 'Leclerc' MBT which is now under development.

ITALY

With 260,000 men Italy, one of the founder members of NATO, would appear on paper to be one of its strongest pillars. In fact the potential of the Italian army in a serious emergency is considerably less than these figures suggest, for several reasons. Defence matters have never been of much interest to the Italian political class, and budget constraints have always been tight.

Even so, some Italian units are of high quality, among them the armoured force. A proportion of their equipment is obsolete, and unlikely to be replaced in the near future; but they can field some first-class assets.

The three army corps are concentrated in the north of the country, the only area favourable to large scale armoured operations. Italy is in the process of disbanding her major armoured formation, the 'Ariete' ('Ram') Armoured Division; but its brigades will be retained, distributed alongside other armoured brigades among the mechanised divisions.

Italy has two armoured brigades equipped with the Leopard 1 — the 'Pozzuolo di Friuli' and 'Centauro' Brigades. The firm of Oto Melara has built 920 Leopard 1 tanks under licence, and they also serve in the tank battalions which are integral to the motorised brigades. The 'Ariete's' brigades are equipped with the M60 A1 Patton, of which Italy has some 300. Territorial units still have some old M47s, but these are being progressively retired from service.

The Italian tank squadron has 15 tanks in three five-tank platoons. Each squadron commander has a tank, as do the regimental commanding officer and second-in-command, giving a regimental strength of 50 tanks.

Like their French comrades, the Italian tankmen look forward to the eventual introduction of a sophisticated new MBT at the end of the century. Oto Melara's projected 'Ariete' tank will have a 1,400hp engine, the latest composite armour, and a smooth-bore 120mm gun. Its arrival will allow the reduction of the tank platoon to four vehicles.

(Right) Leopard 1 A1 of the 'Mantua' Brigade's tank regiment under way on the Celina Medina ranges.

(Below) Tanks are warm, and you don't have to walk — but they are more work to maintain than a pair of boots . . . Repairing a track on an M60 A1 of the 'Ariete' Armoured Division during a firing exercise on Sardinia.

(Above) Men of the 'Mantua' Bde. align their Leopard 1 perfectly for a demonstration in front of NATO senior officers.

(Right) Leopard 1 of the 4th Tank Battalion 'Passalacqua' disembarking from an Iveco tank transporter north of Milan. In wartime the intensive use of tank transporters is vital for armoured units, to keep wear on tracks, engine and crew to a minimum until the last possible moment before 'going tactical'.

Young Italian tank
commander of the
'Passalacqua' Bn. wearing
the Italian tank troopers'
leather protective gear, and
the black beret traditional
among most of the world's
tank units.

(Left) Leopard 1 A1 of the
'Mantua' Bde. moving fast
over the plain in the Celina
Medina range area. The
'Leo 1' can reach a speed of
65km/h (40mph).

65

Printed in Italy

This edition published
in Great Britain 1990 by
Windrow & Greene Ltd
5 Gerrard Street
London W1V 7LJ

Publishers of
'MILITARY ILLUSTRATED Past and Present'

British Library Cataloguing in Publication Data
Debay, Yves
  Allied battle tanks.
  1. Armoured combat vehicles
  I. Title   II. Series
  623.74752

Acknowledgements:
The author wishes to record his sincere
thanks to the officers, non-commissioned
officers and men of the NATO armoured
forces who made him welcome and co-
operated with his photography. In particular
he wishes to thank the public relations
officers of the armoured units of the Danish
armed forces, of 1st British Corps, 1st
Netherlands Corps, 1st (BE) Corps, of I, II
and III Corps of the Bundeswehr, of the
Canadian 4th Brigade Group, of V and VII
Corps of the US Army, of the French
Armoured Mechanised Corps and the Italian
Army; and to extend his gratitude to those
personnel of SHAPE and SIRPA-Terre who
helped make this book possible.